THE
FLEXIBLE WORKPLACE
POCKETBOOK

By Anne Dickens

Drawings by Phil Hailstone

"Goes beyond the theory, and skilfully takes us through the steps needed to ensure successful implementation of flexible working arrangements. An invaluable management resource!"

Moira Williamson, Personnel Manager (Development), Scottish Legal Aid Board

"Anne Dickens has set out, clearly and comprehensively, the whys and hows of flexible working. The reader wi'' ''''' ' benefit from Anne's considerable experience and expertise in helping a ''''''''''''''''''''''''''''''''cessful business outcomes through flexible workin''''''''''''''''''''''''''''''''read."

Lynette Swift, Manag'''''''''''''

Published by:
Management Pocketbooks Ltd
Laurel House, Station Approach, Alresford, Hants SO24 9JH, U.K.
Tel: +44 (0)1962 735573   Fax: +44 (0)1962 733637
E-mail: sales@pocketbook.co.uk
Website: www.pocketbook.co.uk

This edition published 2005.

British Library Cataloguing-in-Publication Data – A catalogue record for this book is available from the British Library.

ISBN 1 903776 40 6

Design, typesetting and graphics by **efex ltd**. Printed in U.K.

CONTENTS

INTRODUCTION

Much is made of culture in organisations. It is, for many people, the single most important thing to get right. It is also a difficult thing to define. If you asked people in your organisation what culture was, they might say:

- *'Our culture is the way we feel about work'*
- *'Our culture is the way we do things here'*
- *'Our culture is what other people think about us'*

It is what your organisation looks and feels like – from the inside. And from the outside.

For me, a major factor influencing organisational culture is the degree of **control** people feel they have. Being in control of their work, and the way they work, helps people to take more responsibility for their input to the business and to the team. In turn they become more self-sufficient, so less needy of management supervision. They feel more empowered and hence more valued as individuals, leading to increased goodwill towards their employer and commitment to the organisation.

By creating a more flexible workplace you can give people a degree of control over their working lives that will change your organisational culture – for good. The next two pages give examples of what others have said after getting a taste of flexibility.

SHREWSBURY
HEALTH LIBRARY
THE LEARNING CENTRE

"I feel far less stressed"

"It's great to get away early and catch the kids now and then"

"There's no such thing as being late any more!"

"I feel empowered – I can make my own decisions"

"Communication between the team is better: the whole team's involved before decisions are taken"

"Lunchtime cover is not an issue any more – there's no dissent or argument"

INTRODUCTION

"There's less bureaucracy"

"We are providing a much better service for our customers"

"My work is more in tune with my body clock"

"I'm in a less frantic state of mind"

"My partner works shifts and the flexibility has made a huge difference to our lives"

"We work closer together generating a better team spirit"

WHAT IS FLEXIBLE WORKING?

WHAT IS FLEXIBLE WORKING?

STRATEGIC CONTEXT

Today's world of work is changing more quickly than ever. More women are now going to work, the population is living longer so our workforce is ageing, and the relationship between families and work is different.

As well as this social change, organisations need to keep pace with technological and legal changes, and respond to ever increasing demands from clients and customers.

The workplace, consequently, needs to change too. Organisations are being encouraged to make their workplaces more flexible so that their employees' working patterns can be adapted to meet business needs.

From the employees' point of view, many are seeking a better work-life balance. That means employers need to respond, if they want to keep their people happy. A better quality of life for employees will have a positive effect on the performance of the business.

WHAT IS FLEXIBLE WORKING?

STRATEGIC CONTEXT

Ten reasons to create a flexible workplace:

1. The workforce is ageing, with an increasing number of employees over 35.

2. Stress in the workplace is a significant cause of sickness absence and reduced productivity.

3. The proportion of women in the workforce is increasing.

4. Graduates are looking for a better work-life balance from new employers.

5. The proportion of the workforce with caring responsibilities – both child and elder care – is increasing.

WHAT IS FLEXIBLE WORKING?

STRATEGIC CONTEXT

Ten reasons to create a flexible workplace:

6. The majority of managers consider that their home life is as important as their work.

7. The Government is increasing legal rights to flexible working for working people with families.

8. The number of workers who are lone parents is growing.

9. Competition for skills and talent amongst companies makes providing attractive work environments important.

10. People from different ethnic and cultural backgrounds, who may require/desire different working patterns, are forming a larger proportion of the workforce.

BETTER BALANCE

Time is a precious commodity. People want to maximise the control they have over the way they use their time.

Flexible working is about recognising individuals' differing needs, different lifestyles, and different life stages and creating an environment in which people can balance time and input inside and outside their work.

Flexible working helps people to create a better balance. If that balance is right, people and teams are healthier, they can be more productive and effective at work, and get more out of life generally.

WHAT IS FLEXIBLE WORKING?

BETTER BALANCE

Of course, the right balance is different for everyone.

For some people, work is a vocation or a passion and they enjoy dedicating a lot of time to it. For others, their leisure activities are important and they want to create as much time as possible away from work.

Your employee might be a volunteer who would like to make a regular commitment to their charity. Or someone with a physical or mental health problem that requires a flexible workplace to facilitate treatment or support. Or perhaps someone's family life is more than usually important to them.

And for many of us, the best balance involves a bit of each of these.

RESPECTING DIFFERENCE

People have different lifestyles, different needs and different dreams. All these factors combine in different ways to make up a workforce of individuals with unique requirements in relation to their work-life balance and need for flexibility.

As managers, we need to **avoid making value judgements** about the different views people have about what makes a good work-life balance.

FLEXIBLE WORKING PATTERNS

Flexible working options are many and varied. They are explained in more detail in Flexible Solutions (pages 37-64). They involve an organisation changing **where**, **when** and **how** its employees work. They encompass a variety of different working patterns including:

 Flexible working time – where a person's total hours are worked at different times in the day. For example, an employee might be allowed to arrive at any time in the morning and leave at any time in the evening, provided they work their contracted hours

 Flexible working hours – where the total number of hours someone works is varied. For example, a person may work only three days each week and be paid pro rata accordingly

 Flexible career – where someone takes a break in their career, but remains an employee. For example, an employee may take a year away from work unpaid, to pursue a leisure activity, and take up the same employment on return

 Flexible place – where a person is based somewhere other than the organisation's office to do their work. For example, if someone has a job that takes them out and about, there might be no need for a permanent office base

THE BUSINESS CASE

THE BUSINESS CASE

WHO BENEFITS?

Organisations from every sector are facing increasing demands from all quarters and need to find ways to optimise performance.

Public sector bodies are required to meet targets and report on key performance indicators. The quest for profit in the private sector is never ceasing. And in the not-for-profit and charitable sectors, the competition for income is tougher than ever.

On top of this, customers, clients and service users want better and more accessible services and products.

THE MANAGER'S ROLE

As a manager, your role is about helping your organisation to succeed through its people. Flexible working is one of the tools you have at your disposal to help your team perform effectively.

If an organisation's people are happy and committed, then creativity, efficiency and productivity improve. This in turn, has a positive impact on all-round performance, ultimately benefiting the client.

BUSINESS BENEFITS TRIANGLE

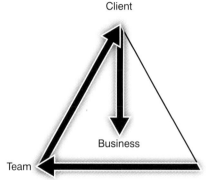

Client

Business

Team

Individual

By creating an environment where people are able to work flexibly, you can create a Win Win Win situation for everyone concerned.

BENEFITS TO THE INDIVIDUAL

Many of us are living pressured and stressful lives. We have 24/7 shopping and communications and our working lives are subject to constant change and upheaval.

Family structures are also changing, with many children having both parents at work.

Striking the right balance between our work and home lives is one way we can regain some control over our lives.

THE BUSINESS CASE

BENEFITS TO THE INDIVIDUAL

FLEXIBILITY

A flexible workplace is the starting point for many people in the search for good work-life balance.

- Even a small element of flexibility in **when** or **where** they work can enable people more easily to deal with issues and problems that arise outside work. This in turn frees them up to concentrate on their job when they are in the workplace
- Routine household chores may be difficult to fulfil if someone has a long journey to and from work
- Looking after young children, or elderly or sick relatives is demanding of time and energy and can be unpredictable, requiring flexibility
- Hobbies, voluntary commitments and other leisure activities are important to us all

By creating a flexible workplace, you will start to help your employees create a better work-life balance for themselves and those around them.

BENEFITS TO THE INDIVIDUAL

EMPOWERMENT

Control is crucially important. By taking, or being given, some control over our working lives, we will in turn feel empowered.

- How often do we hear people complain about their managers, or about company rules? By allowing people to take control of where, how and when they work, we enable them to **take responsibility** for their work and **be accountable** for their actions and outputs. This helps to build trust between managers and their staff and contributes towards a productive healthy working relationship

- The amount of control individuals have over all aspects of their lives is recognised as a key factor in their health and well-being

By giving your employees the responsibility to organise their own working days according to agreed parameters, you effectively give them more control over their lives.

THE BUSINESS CASE

BENEFITS TO THE INDIVIDUAL
ENHANCED SKILLS

If people feel in control, and can take more responsibility for their work, they will invest more in it.

- To work flexibly and be successful, employees need to develop new skills. Things like time management, project management, effective planning and good communications are all pre-requisites of flexible working. The desire for flexibility encourages new learning

- Developing new skills takes time and effort. Feeling as though they have more time gives people the opportunity to take changes on board and develop new skills accordingly. Taking the pressure off also allows people scope for thinking time and creativity

- Some organisations may require high-level specialist skills for a temporary period, so flexible employment can help fill that temporary skills gap

By building a flexible work environment you are enabling people to develop skills which will make them personally more effective.

BENEFITS TO THE INDIVIDUAL
WELL-BEING

Our physical and mental health are vital to our overall work effort.

- People's health is affected by stressful and pressured working environments, where working hours do not fit with home lives and responsibilities, or where lack of trust is both disempowering and demotivating

- For some people, aligning work to their personal body clocks makes them happier, healthier and more productive

- Many busy working parents cite the need for *me-time*. Not family time, but time dedicated to that individual for leisure, for health, or for spiritual relaxation and renewal

BENEFITS TO THE INDIVIDUAL

WELL-BEING (Cont'd)

- Stress in the workplace is a growing phenomenon. **It suppresses productivity**. It is a growing cause of sickness absence and an alarmingly common reason for employers being taken to employment tribunal. Overall, it is a formidable enemy for any organisation

A flexible workplace can help to create the time and space to ensure that it is also a healthy one.

BENEFITS TO THE INDIVIDUAL

IMPROVED MORALE

Healthy morale amongst the workforce is the *holy grail* for an enlightened manager. But morale is a nebulous concept – impossible to define precisely and with a different meaning for different people.

Your employees' morale is both affected by, and has an effect on, the culture of the organisation.

THE BUSINESS CASE

BENEFITS TO THE INDIVIDUAL
IMPROVED MORALE (Cont'd)

Crucial to healthy morale is enjoyment of the job and respect for colleagues. To enjoy a job people must be motivated and committed and have the skills and confidence to deliver the expected outcomes. Feeling trusted and empowered provides that confidence. People need to be in a position where they can manage their own workload and be judged by the outputs.

Healthy morale leads to goodwill towards the organisation and a commitment to get the job done.

By creating a flexible workplace, you will make a positive impact on these key issues.

BENEFITS TO THE INDIVIDUAL

Improved morale:
- Goodwill
- Motivation
- Commitment
- Job satisfaction

Well-being:
- Physical health
- Reduced stress
- Me-time
- Work to body clock

More flexibility:
- Leisure
- Household chores
- Care commitments
- Work-life balance

...to the individual

Enhanced skills:
- Time management
- Creativity
- Communications
- Better planning

Empowerment:
- Control
- Responsibility
- Accountability
- Trust

BENEFITS TO THE TEAM

If the individuals within a team are each happier and empowered, this will naturally impact positively on the team. Specifically, the work involved at team level to develop a flexible workplace can provide a catalyst for improved team working, even before the scheme itself is introduced.

For example, sharing information about work-life balance requirements helps to build mutual empathy and consideration. This in turn improves collective understanding of the team's strengths and limitations, which can create further support and flexibility.

By allowing team members to work together to develop flexible solutions which suit their needs, the team is more likely to take ownership of the solution. And because working flexibly requires effective and focused team communication, more disciplined and organised planning and reporting, and a sharing of skills and information, the whole team will become more efficient, effective and productive. Secondary benefits, such as self-reflection, refined business systems, and innovation may also start to develop.

BENEFITS TO THE TEAM

More productive

Information shared

Better, more effective team working

Happier team

Empathy

...to the team

Better communications

More discipline

Mutual trust

Mutual support

Team in control

Enhanced team skills

Consideration for colleagues

BENEFITS TO THE CLIENT

Your client is what your organisation should be focused on.

Whether you offer a service or a product, directly or indirectly, free of charge or paid for, your clients' experiences will be a reflection of the quality of service you offer. And that client experience will flow, in part, from the exchanges they have had with your staff.

Contact with happy, committed, knowledgeable employees will make a positive impact on your clients and make them feel that they have received good service. A happy personal interaction between two people can even, in certain circumstances, compensate for a service or product deficiency.

By creating a flexible workplace, you may also extend your business hours, or the hours during which clients have access to your services.

BENEFITS TO THE CLIENT

Happier contacts:
- Better informed
- More responsive

Better access:
- Extended hours
- Better cover
- Timely responses

...to the client

Improved service:
- Enhanced quality
- More knowledgeable
- More adaptable

Enhanced loyalty:
- Repeat business
- Quality relationships

BENEFITS TO THE BUSINESS

Ultimately, it is the overall business which benefits from a flexible workplace.

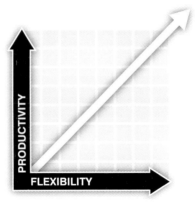

BENEFITS TO THE BUSINESS

INTERNAL FACTORS

Staff

It is important to recruit and retain the right people from the outset and then to help them build the right attitudes and skills. People rate flexibility alongside salary, so flexible working can increase loyalty to your organisation and improve retention. It will also reduce lateness and sickness absence and associated costs.

Workplace & systems

The pressure to compete or to meet targets can often mean that new ways of working have to be found to make the best use of staff, other resources and equipment. To introduce flexible working, managers need to ensure systems are efficient and management information is sound. Where organisations have peaks and troughs in demand, a flexible workplace can help deal with that fluctuation.

Culture

If managers can delegate to their teams the responsibility for organising the working day and workload, this will free them up from their supervisory roles. They can then be the leaders and coaches we want them to be which, in turn, will affect their confidence and behaviour. A climate of trust and empowerment will soon reap its own rewards in the form of a more adaptable, flexible and creative workforce.

BENEFITS TO THE BUSINESS

EXTERNAL FACTORS

Productivity

Employees are a key factor in any organisation's productivity and profitability. A flexible workforce in a flexible workplace will have a positive impact on your organisation's key targets. Retaining the right people also reduces the very high cost – in financial and people terms – of recruitment.

Clients

How many of your clients and customers work traditional 9-5 hours? Not many these days. Workforce flexibility helps organisations of all shapes and sizes to respond and adapt to changing market conditions and client demands. Client satisfaction is increased and complaints are reduced, leading to repeat business and loyalty.

Reputation

Employment law increasingly favours working parents, and employers must adapt accordingly. It also requires equality and encourages diversity; a flexible workplace enables an organisation to attract and appoint from a broader range of candidates. Best practice in employment reflects positively on your organisation's reputation.

BENEFITS TO THE BUSINESS

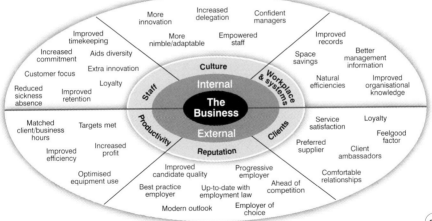

THE BUSINESS CASE

BENEFITS TO THE BUSINESS

'Our survey* respondents have demonstrated that they are looking to their employers and the Government to provide a working climate that enables them to make changes without impacting on their career success or their earnings potential.

With the labour market becoming more female, older and more diverse, these are growing demands that the Government is already starting to respond to - and that all employers need to sit up and listen to. The UK's demographics are already changing: the workplace cannot afford not to.'

www.employersandwork-lifebalance.org.uk

FLEXIBLE SOLUTIONS

THE OPTIONS

There is a range of different flexible working patterns and approaches to choose from. Examples of all of these may be found in operation in different types of organisations. Not all of these patterns suit every person or every type of job. It is important to understand the individual's requirements and the nature of their work, and to choose a solution which balances both these needs.

Options for flexible working fall broadly into four categories:

 Flexible **working time** – where a person's total hours are worked at different times in the day

 Flexible **career** – where someone takes a break in their career, but remains an employee

 Flexible **working hours** – where the total number of hours someone works is varied

 Flexible **place** – where a person works from somewhere other than the organisation's office

FLEXIBLE SOLUTIONS

FLEXIBLE WORKING TIME

Flexible working time enables a person to work at different times in the day.

In practice the flexibility a scheme offers varies, depending on the type of that scheme and the rules that are applied.

The following are examples of flexible working time schemes:

- Flexitime
- Compressed hours
- Annualised hours
- Shift working

FLEXIBLE SOLUTIONS

FLEXIBLE WORKING TIME

FLEXITIME

Flexitime schemes give employees choice about the times of day they work, allowing them to vary their start, finish and break times.

These schemes can vary considerably. A relatively limited scheme allows employees with a 40 hours per week contract to work between 8am and 6pm, with lunch to be taken between 12pm and 2pm. A more flexible scheme might enable people to complete their total hours any time between 6am and 9pm each day, with the freedom to choose the time of their lunch break.

Many flexitime schemes have agreed *core* hours when everyone is expected to be at work. Ideally, these core hours should coincide with the busiest times of day for your business. Core hours are not essential, but mean that everyone is in the office at certain times of the day, which can be useful for meetings, etc.

Schemes can also allow for the accumulation of extra hours worked over set periods, within agreed parameters. These can be taken as additional days off. Effectively, the sky is the limit for flexitime schemes – it depends entirely on your business.

FLEXIBLE WORKING TIME

FLEXITIME

Benefits	Challenges
Extends coverage across the day, broadening access times for clients	May require additional building and systems support at both ends of the day
Facilitates matching work times with peaks and troughs in workload demand	May require the introduction of a time monitoring system to log hours worked
Travel outside traditional peak hours can reduce journey times	Some additional manager time may be required to monitor scheme
Allows people to balance personal and work commitments	High workload can create unsustainable accumulation of additional hours
Works with individual's body clock for greater efficiency and productivity	Can lead to clock-watching
Allows the accumulation of credit hours to be taken as days off	
Reduces unpunctuality	

FLEXIBLE WORKING TIME

COMPRESSED HOURS

A compressed working hours scheme allows employees to work their total number of contracted hours over a shortened period of time, by increasing the hours worked every day.

For example, employees might work their full weekly hours over four days, rather than five. Alternatively they might work nine days each fortnight instead of ten.

FLEXIBLE SOLUTIONS

FLEXIBLE WORKING TIME

COMPRESSED HOURS

Benefits	Challenges
Extends coverage across the day, broadening access times for clients	May require additional building and systems support at both ends of the day
Enables employees to have time away from work during the week	It is necessary to plan ahead to ensure coverage every day
Allows people to plan for increased blocks of personal time	Difficult to manage unexpected demand as full team not always available
Retains full-time salary whilst providing larger portions of non-work time	Longer working days can be difficult for people to sustain over the long term
May create quiet time at either end of the day	Compressing the workload into fewer days can be stressful
Travel outside traditional peak hours can reduce journey times	May require re-working of leave allowance and sickness absence calculations

FLEXIBLE WORKING TIME
ANNUALISED HOURS

Working time is organised so that the pattern of work for a whole year is established to meet organisational or employee needs.

This scheme is normally used to fit in with peaks and troughs of work over the year. Effectively, this means that the majority of a person's contracted hours might be worked during a particular season, eg in the farming sector at harvest time, with little or no work at other times.

It can be used in other sectors with less extreme contrasts, eg in finance departments to assist with the preparation of end of year accounts over a, typically, three month period each year, without resorting to the payment of overtime.

To assist with employee cash flow, monthly income may be spread over the year. Alternatively, it can be adjusted to match the hours worked in each agreed period.

FLEXIBLE WORKING TIME

ANNUALISED HOURS

Benefits	Challenges
Allows for coverage of predictable peaks and troughs in demand	May be complex to manage and administer
Service can be closely matched to client demand	Deficits and credits in hours need to be addressed when contracts cease
The necessity for overtime is reduced	The potential unpredictability of irregular hours can be disruptive
Can create maximum flexibility for staff	In some organisations, less opportunity for overtime is a disincentive

FLEXIBLE SOLUTIONS

FLEXIBLE WORKING TIME

SHIFT WORKING

Shifts give employers the scope to have their business open for longer periods, up to a 24 hour, 7 day a week operation. This is typically how the UK emergency and health services operate. Shifts are also prominent in certain manufacturing environments.

Employees work agreed shift patterns of, say, 8, 10 or 12 hours over planned periods, with breaks and rest days built in as appropriate.

Payment of a premium for unsocial hours may be required, although a parallel commitment to flexible working arrangements may mitigate that need.

FLEXIBLE WORKING TIME

SHIFT WORKING

Benefits	Challenges
Enables the ultimate 24/7 coverage	Requires careful forward planning to dovetail coverage
Gives certainty of working patterns to employees	If a continuous operation is paramount, some contingency may be required
Potential for employees to rest for long break periods between shifts	Perpetuates inflexible hours of work for employees
Unsocial hours pay premiums can be attractive	Requires punctuality for handovers
	Can involve unsocial hours with associated pay premiums

FLEXIBLE SOLUTIONS

FLEXIBLE WORKING HOURS

Flexible working hours means that people increase or, more often, reduce the hours they are contracted to work.

These are effectively part-time based schemes, though their shape and the driving forces behind them may vary considerably.

The following are examples of flexible working hours schemes:

- Part-time working
- Term-time working
- Job share

FLEXIBLE SOLUTIONS

FLEXIBLE WORKING HOURS

PART-TIME WORKING

Part-time working is a means for people to work less than the standard contractual hours. This may involve working fewer full-time days, or shorter working days, eg mornings only, or a combination of both.

It is important to recognise that reduced hours equals, basically speaking, reduced capacity. An employee should not be expected to carry out the equivalent of a full-time workload on a part-time contract.

This is particularly important when an existing employee, eg someone returning from maternity leave, moves from a full-time to a part-time contract. A reduction in the workload commensurate with the reduced hours should also be made.

FLEXIBLE SOLUTIONS

FLEXIBLE WORKING HOURS

PART-TIME WORKING

Benefits	Challenges
Service can be closely matched to client demand	Ensuring workload matches contracted hours
May be used to manage budget constraints while avoiding job losses	Other benefits will need to be adjusted pro rata to reflect part-time post
Covers situations where workload insufficient to justify full-time post	Ensuring part-time employees can access support and benefits, eg training
Increases workforce deployment flexibility	

FLEXIBLE WORKING HOURS

PART-TIME WORKING (Cont'd)

Benefits	Challenges
Helps fulfil equal opportunities requirements and diverse workforce needs	Finding times when everyone is available for meetings
Enables employees to fulfil caring responsibilities more easily	Extensive use leads to an increased headcount with associated costs
Enables those who can only work part-time, eg health treatment needs, to be in employment	
Can be used to phase someone towards retirement	

FLEXIBLE WORKING HOURS

TERM-TIME WORKING (PARENTS' HOURS)

Term-time working makes it possible for permanent employees to take unpaid leave during school holiday periods.

This enables employers to recruit parents who want to work but who find it difficult to do so when their children are on holiday.

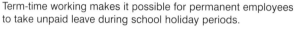

FLEXIBLE SOLUTIONS

FLEXIBLE WORKING HOURS
TERM-TIME WORKING (PARENTS' HOURS)

Benefits	Challenges
Increases potential to recruit and retain working parents	Finding short-term cover for holiday periods can be difficult
Enables retention of key skills, which you may have invested heavily in	Requires forward planning to organise work schedules
Solves childcare problems during school holidays	Can place a burden on remaining staff
Helps fulfil equal opportunities requirements	Loss of salary for non-working periods

FLEXIBLE WORKING HOURS

JOB SHARE

In job share arrangements, the responsibilities of a full-time job are shared between two employees employed on a part-time basis. These two people work together to cover the duties of a post normally done by one full-time person. The responsibilities may be divided between the sharers, or sometimes specific projects or clients are allocated to each sharer.

If a job is completely split between two people, then two part-time posts have effectively been created.

Both job-sharers receive pay for the hours they work. Holidays and other benefits are awarded pro rata.

FLEXIBLE SOLUTIONS

FLEXIBLE WORKING HOURS

JOB SHARE

Benefits	Challenges
Two brains and skill sets applied to one job	Ensuring adequate handover when responsibilities are shared
Creates a wider knowledge and skills base in your organisation	Work continuity may be difficult to achieve
Cover for absence may be easier, as holidays are planned and coincidental sickness is unlikely	Extensive use leads to an increased headcount with associated costs – can increase cost of single post
Can reduce stress through problem sharing and solving	Reviewing post and workload when one sharer leaves may be difficult
Can increase creativity through joint working and brainstorming	Additional member of staff to manage
Can result in a high work output	

FLEXIBLE CAREER OPTIONS

Flexible career options provide a means of managing relationships between employers and employees during periods when people want to take a break from their jobs, thus enabling the employer to retain valuable skills and experience.

- Career breaks/sabbaticals – extended unpaid periods away from work for any criteria in the employer's scheme

- Unpaid leave – occasional short periods of unpaid leave

- Carer leave – to facilitate carer responsibilities

- Study leave – to support staff who are pursuing personal and/or career development by providing time off for study

FLEXIBLE SOLUTIONS

FLEXIBLE PLACE OPTIONS

Location-flexible options create opportunities for employees to work somewhere other than in the main office. This means having the equipment and the systems to work from remote locations.

This solution might be in response to a job which can more easily be done from elsewhere or driven by the need to reduce overheads and save accommodation costs.

The following are examples of flexible place options:

- Homeworking
- Telecentre working
- Mobile working

FLEXIBLE PLACE OPTIONS

HOMEWORKING

Homeworking, as it sounds, enables employees to work from their own homes.

This can typically occur in three ways:

- Ad hoc – as required, eg to concentrate on a particular report or project

- Regular – an arrangement where someone works from home on agreed days each week or month

- Permanent – where an employee's permanent work base is their home

I'll check with production and get straight back to you

FLEXIBLE SOLUTIONS

FLEXIBLE PLACE OPTIONS

HOMEWORKING

Benefits	Challenges
Reduces/eliminates travel time and costs and associated stress	Extra effort is needed to maintain team contact and communications
Enables concentration on task at hand	Work continuity may be difficult to achieve
Creates opportunity to dovetail domestic chores	Difficulty scheduling meetings and group activities
Can improve retention and diversity as it helps people with mobility or caring needs	Investment in health and safety, equipment and furniture costs
Office overheads reduced	Team identity and cohesion can be more difficult to maintain
Accommodation/space needs reduced	Management and supervision from a distance more difficult
Can result in a high work output	Work outputs more difficult to measure

FLEXIBLE PLACE OPTIONS

TELECENTRE WORKING

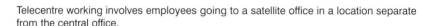

Telecentre working involves employees going to a satellite office in a location separate from the central office.

A telecentre office is typically designed for this purpose and may comprise only basic office requirements. It will usually accommodate workers from a variety of organisations.

This may be a variation on homeworking or it may be used in combination with homeworking or mobile working.

Telecentres can provide *drop in* or *short stay* facilities.

The benefits and challenges are similar to homeworking, but some are unique to this type of working.

FLEXIBLE SOLUTIONS

FLEXIBLE PLACE OPTIONS

TELECENTRE WORKING

Benefits	Challenges
An alternative to homeworking where the home is not a suitable work environment	Still requires some travelling time and expense
Telecentres may be strategically placed to suit the business	Costs of renting or establishing the telecentre
Potentially re-creates the element of social interactivity gained within a traditional office environment	Difficulty scheduling meetings and group activities
Can be strategically situated close to suppliers/clients	Management and supervision from a distance more difficult
There are economies of scale relating to the cost of technology	Work outputs more difficult to measure

FLEXIBLE PLACE OPTIONS

MOBILE WORKING

A mobile worker has no permanent base, and can take advantage of modern technology to work while on the move.

A mobile worker is anyone who is working away from a fixed, office–based place of work for some or all of the time. This may also include people who work from home for some or all of the time.

Many jobs demand mobility, eg traffic wardens, police officers, surveyors, sales representatives. But the advent of mobile technology means that many other jobs can be transformed more effectively into mobile positions.

FLEXIBLE SOLUTIONS

FLEXIBLE PLACE OPTIONS

MOBILE WORKING

Benefits	Challenges
Employees can be highly responsive to client and business needs	Ensure comfort and health and safety of employees
Working in real time – constant contact with and updating of information and systems	Difficulty scheduling meetings and group activities
Time spent travelling between appointments/jobs can be utilised productively	Management and supervision from a distance more difficult
Maximising use of modern technology	Work outputs more difficult to measure

FLEXIBLE SOLUTIONS

SUMMARY

Remember, it is important to ensure that the type of flexible scheme that is chosen balances the needs of the business with the needs of the individual.

Some jobs don't suit certain types of schemes. For example, it is unlikely that it would be possible for a person working as a receptionist to be based at home. However, it might be possible for the receptionist role to be a job shared, to enable two people to work flexibly and to ensure that your reception is covered during an extended working day. This would suit the business, provide your clients with a good service, and provide flexible roles for two people.

WHICH APPROACH?

ADOPTING A STRATEGY

It is possible to introduce flexibility in the workplace in a number of different ways. These include:

- Across the organisation
- On a team-by-team basis
- On an individual basis

The right route for you will depend on your organisation.

ACROSS THE ORGANISATION

Introducing flexibility **across the organisation** means that you develop and implement a scheme which is then applied in the same way to everyone.

For example, some organisations have flexitime schemes that all employees have access to. Others operate shift systems for all staff.

Pros	Cons
Simplicity – a single scheme is more easily understood.	**Inflexible** – a 'one size fits all' scheme may not meet staff needs.
Equality – everyone has access to the same scheme.	**Cumbersome** – is usually centrally administered and creates work.
Leverage – is organisation-wide so can be driven across the organisation.	**Entrenched** – is hard to change or cease once established.
Single system – may require minimum investment.	**Maintenance** – may require substantial software/hardware updates.

TEAM-BY-TEAM

Introducing flexibility on a team-by-team basis means that you invite teams to develop flexible workplace schemes which fit their local business needs, within defined corporate parameters and principles.

For example, some organisations enable different teams to operate different schemes, such as compressed hours in one team and flexible hours in another.

Pros	Cons
Customer focused – responds directly to team's customer service needs.	**Proliferation** – each team will have its own particular approach.
Accountability – encourages co-operation and makes teams take responsibility for their scheme.	**Inconsistency** – can create an inconsistent approach to flexible working across the organisation.
Tailor-made – meets team's specific needs.	**Manager reliant** – requires enlightened and supportive managers.

WHICH APPROACH?

FOR INDIVIDUALS

Introducing flexibility for individuals means that you develop a suite of flexible workplace solutions at a corporate level, but allow individual employees to pick and choose the scheme that suits them, whether it is to work part-time or compressed hours.

Pros	Cons
Nimble – schemes may be started or stopped with minimum consultation.	**Poor accountability** – employees may become very individually focused.
People focused – individuals can adopt schemes which suit their personal circumstances.	**Inequality** – can lead to a first-come-first-served policy with individuals getting preferential treatment.
	Non-cooperation – one person's flexibility may be another's confinement.
	Unempowered managers – can reduce managers' ability and tools for managing individuals.

WHICH APPROACH?

BALANCING RIGHTS AND RESPONSIBILITIES

Many of your employees have a statutory right to ask for changes in their working pattern or location.

Equally, the employer has the right to refuse a request where it would be inappropriate or where a business case can be made against the request.

Ideally, employees need to consider the interests of colleagues and clients when they review their own need for flexibility. The employer should consider all requests for changes in working patterns carefully, but ultimately has a responsibility to its clients to fulfil its duties efficiently and effectively.

Whichever approach is adopted, a balance needs to be struck between the rights and responsibilities of employees and employers when considering the introduction of flexible working schemes.

WHICH APPROACH?

10 PRINCIPLES FOR FLEXIBLE WORKING

Whichever model you adopt to introduce flexible working, it is helpful to have clearly agreed and understood guiding principles.

If your staff are going to move towards a new way of working together, some basic principles will underpin this transition and help guide decision making. Any organisational change can cause stress and uncertainty. It is helpful for people to have a framework within which they can make changes.

A set of guiding principles will also aid troubleshooting when problems arise. Better to anticipate potential pitfalls early and design your flexible workplace with them in mind, rather than allow a scheme to fail because of an unforeseen *elephant trap*.

The aim is to create a clear understanding of the nature of your commitment to a more flexible workplace and to help ensure a fair and consistent approach across the organisation.

WHICH APPROACH?

10 PRINCIPLES FOR FLEXIBLE WORKING

The following principles have been developed to underpin the introduction of new ways of working. They reflect the sort of issues you should consider. They should be able to be adapted to work in any type of organisation but, naturally, yours may require fewer, more, or different principles, to suit your particular circumstances.

1 Business first

The needs of the business are the primary consideration. Ultimately everyone is working to make the business successful. Any other approach is self-defeating.

2 Fairness

Everyone has a right to have their need for flexible working considered, while at the same time recognising that not all solutions will be right for every person or every team's business needs.

10 PRINCIPLES FOR FLEXIBLE WORKING

❸ Consistency

Support and encourage all managers across your organisation to create flexibility for their teams, so as to support the principle of fairness.

❹ Local decision-making

Managers and teams are the best judge of their particular business and individual needs. Aim for locally invented and locally implemented flexible workplace solutions.

❺ Communication and involvement

Commit to involving people in the development of a flexible workplace (your team, your colleagues and your customers) and to communicating new schemes.

❻ Innovation

Encourage creative thinking so as to develop relevant and workable solutions and to make the flexible workplace a success.

10 PRINCIPLES FOR FLEXIBLE WORKING

7 Consensus

Aim for consensus within each team about the kind of flexible solution to adopt and the details of that scheme. Listen to ideas, be open-minded and be prepared to change your mind.

8 Respect

Respect other people's needs and ideas. Don't make value judgements. Acknowledge others have lives different from your own. Be objective and open to change.

9 Monitoring and measurement

Focus on the business impact of your new way of working by developing success criteria and monitoring and measurement systems.

10 Trust

Trust each other: to adhere to these principles, to make the team mutually supportive and to ensure your flexible workplace is a success.

CHOOSING A SCHEME

Many organisations deploy a suite of flexible working options from which staff can choose.

This might comprise a combination of options, involving when and where staff choose to work, and might include the opportunity to work from home and to take a sabbatical after an appropriate length of service. Indeed, your organisation's portfolio of flexible workplace options might include all of those listed on page 14.

The decision about whether a team or an individual can work flexibly will depend on associated corporate rules or guidelines for each scheme, or on the employee's manager.

CHOOSING A SCHEME

Issues to take into account when drawing up such guidelines include:

The nature of the business – The type of work your organisation is in will have a major bearing on the type of flexibility you can introduce. Eg, if your business provides a service to the public and they have access to your building, or if you have a production operation, you may require constant cover.

The job – Generally any job which can be managed by objectives and defined outputs may be adapted to some kind of flexible workplace. But not every type of flexibility is suitable for every job, eg you are unlikely to be able to have a shop assistant or an assembly line operator working from home! Consideration should also be given to the impact on and inter-relationship with other jobs.

The person – Not everyone wants or is able to work flexibly. Often an irregular working day or location means reduced contact and communication. Consider also individuals' preferred working styles (are they self-motivated, self-disciplined?); their time management; their need for peer company; line management, etc.

CHOOSING A SCHEME

Management and supervision – Consider what impact the flexible workplace will have on the management and supervision procedures in your team. Flexibility within a team will usually result in less *hands on* management. It is likely to require a performance management style which is based on clear objectives and plans and assessment of outputs. Also consider any special training and support needs of your staff.

Time management – New systems may be needed to track the hours worked by employees. Sickness absence and annual leave calculations may need to be reviewed and varied to ensure they are practicable in your flexible workplace.

Appraisal and reward – You may need to introduce new systems to monitor work and to judge performance. You may also wish to consider developing systems which reward flexibility.

Communication – Continued regular communications within and between teams may become more difficult. You may need to establish new communication systems to replicate team meetings, one-to-ones, etc.

CHOOSING A SCHEME

Equipment – A flexible workplace might mean new software and supporting systems, eg a new time recording system or on-line discussion forum. Make sure people receive sufficient training in any new systems and equipment. There may also be associated costs.

Health and safety – Consider whether any health and safety procedures are compromised with the introduction of flexible working. This is particularly important when considering home or mobile working.

Security – Policies relating to confidentiality of information, access to data and IT equipment, and general office security should be reviewed.

Contracts – Provided both sides are in agreement, the employee's contract may need to be varied to take account of the new arrangements.

ENCOURAGING
FLEXIBLE BEHAVIOUR

WHAT DOES FLEXIBILITY FEEL LIKE?

Typically, we use the word *culture* to describe what a place feels like to work in. The culture in a flexible organisation may feel very different from that in less flexible places. This is because making the transition to a more flexible workplace calls for a change in management and team behaviours.

WHAT DOES FLEXIBILITY FEEL LIKE?

CHARACTERISTICS

Typical cultural characteristics of a flexible workplace include:

- People feel empowered to get on with their work, knowing that they have the support of their manager and will be judged against agreed criteria

- Organisational systems are designed to support the people and the work so that they liberate managers, as opposed to being cumbersome, time-consuming or self-perpetuating

- Information is regarded as a key asset and is shared; there is a feeling of openness and transparency and team communication is planned and frequent

WHAT DOES FLEXIBILITY FEEL LIKE?

CHARACTERISTICS (Cont'd)

- People take responsibility for their work and are comfortable being held to account for its delivery
- Everyone's preferred work-life balance is taken seriously so that different people may have different working patterns while all contributing to the same organisational project
- Teams are self-sustaining and team members are mutually aware and supportive
- There is trust between managers and individuals

SUPPORTING THE CHANGE

Making the transition to a more flexible workplace calls for a change in management and team behaviour, leading to a different organisational culture. As you will have recognised, many of these behaviours are those associated generally with effective people and performance management.

This model shows the inter-relationship between management style and flexibility.

	Controlling	**Empowering**
Flexible	**Frustration** Limited output	**Freedom to perform** Maximum output
Inflexible	**Demotivation** Minimum output	**Clock-watching** Limited output

WORKPLACE

MANAGERS

ENCOURAGING FLEXIBLE BEHAVIOUR

SUPPORTING THE CHANGE

If your workplace is inflexible and your managers do not delegate, people will soon become demotivated, resentful and ineffective.

Having either empowering managers or a flexible workplace may bring some benefits, but limits the scope for significant improvement in performance and culture change. Effective managers without the organisational flexibility to delegate control over working patterns to their staff, will not be in a position to use their skills to maximum advantage. This will lead to frustration and disillusionment. A flexible workplace full of inflexible managers creates a culture of clock-watching and self-absorption.

Introducing flexibility is not enough. By supporting an enlightened approach to management, you will support the immediate implementation of change and ensure your new flexible workplace is sustainable over the long term.

ENCOURAGING FLEXIBLE BEHAVIOUR

SUPPORTING THE CHANGE

Consider some of the attributes of flexible and inflexible managers:

Flexible management style	Inflexible management style
Share business objectives with your team.	Keep business objectives close to your chest and change them as you see fit.
Delegate responsibility and authority for work to be done.	Closely supervise people's work on a daily basis.
Agree project plans with milestones for checking.	Regularly expect people to make last minute adjustments to their work.
Be clear about expected outputs and outcomes at the outset.	Judge success by number of hours worked.
Promote and encourage openness and communication about business issues.	Fail to share business information.
Champion flexibility and ensure good work-life balance.	Judge commitment by long hours at work.
Allow people to record and be accountable for their hours worked.	Closely monitor hours worked.

SUPPORTING THE CHANGE

Where are you on the flexibility scale?

VERY FLEXIBLE   VERY INFLEXIBLE

ENCOURAGING FLEXIBLE BEHAVIOUR

SUPPORTING THE CHANGE
WORKSHOPS

If you feel you and your colleagues need some help to
make the change, consider running workshops
to help build the skills and confidence
required. These might be for everyone or
just for the key people involved.

The following pages contain some
ideas for workshop exercises
which you might adapt to suit
your team or organisation.

ENCOURAGING FLEXIBLE BEHAVIOUR

SUPPORTING THE CHANGE

EXERCISE 1

Understanding individual work-life balance

Aim of the exercise

To highlight individuals' work-life balance issues and to generate a sense of self and mutual understanding. This leads naturally to an appreciation of the potential benefits of flexible working.

Method

Each person is given a copy of the work-life balance wheel and asked:

1. To plot the importance to them of each segment in blue pen
2. To plot their current situation in red pen

Discuss the variances for everyone between their ideal work-life balance and the reality. In particular, highlight the barriers to change and consider how introducing a more flexible workplace might help people move more toward their ideal.

ENCOURAGING FLEXIBLE BEHAVIOUR

SUPPORTING THE CHANGE
EXERCISE 1

Notes

You can vary the contents of the segments to suit your team.

It is not the aim of this exercise to create a perfect circle of any size. This is not a value judgement of different people's lives, preferences or priorities. It is very likely that the shape resulting from each person's plotting will be irregular. It is also probable that this shape will be different at different times in people's lives.

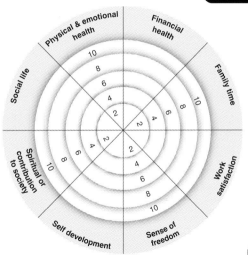

ENCOURAGING FLEXIBLE BEHAVIOUR

SUPPORTING THE CHANGE
EXERCISE 2

Understanding the business case

Aim of the exercise
To help people to identify and understand the business advantages of the flexible workplace and the benefits it brings to the different parts of the organisation.

Method
Form into three groups. Ask each group to discuss the potential benefits of more flexible working to a different part of the organisation:

- **Individuals:** What would individuals gain from a more flexible workplace?
- **Team:** How do teams benefit, how are they more effective?
- **Client:** What do your organisation's clients gain?

ENCOURAGING FLEXIBLE BEHAVIOUR

SUPPORTING THE CHANGE
EXERCISE 2

Understanding the business case

Method (Cont'd)
Each group nominates a scribe and
reporter. After discussion, the groups feed
back their responses under each of the
three headings. The facilitator then leads a
discussion to identify how the advantages
gained under these headings lead to
general business benefits. These are
captured alongside the advantages
previously identified to demonstrate the
broader positive impact that increased
flexibility can have.

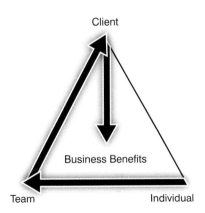

Notes
Refer to pages 20-33, *The Business Case* for prompts to get ideas flowing if necessary.

ENCOURAGING FLEXIBLE BEHAVIOUR

SUPPORTING THE CHANGE
EXERCISE 3

Building success!

Aim of the exercise
To identify the barriers to change and a route to your successful flexible workplace.

Method
In pairs, each places a 'metaphorical' hat on their head:

The Dreamer thinks what the flexible workplace would look like in an ideal situation. How would it feel for you as an individual? What positive things would it do for you and the organisation? What would the benefits be?, etc.

The Critic sees the difficulties and obstacles to the flexible workplace. What are the barriers to making it work? What could go wrong?, etc.

SUPPORTING THE CHANGE

EXERCISE 3

Building success!

Encourage people to visualise themselves as the advocate of the stance they have taken and to stay in their chosen role. Once enough time has elapsed, get Dreamers to make the case for the flexible workplace and then get Critics to knock it down. Once both sides have been aired, ask the Dreamer and Critic pairs to work together to become success Architects!

The Architect can see how to make it happen. What would need to be done to optimise the opportunities and benefits and minimise the barriers and risks? What procedures would need to be in place to facilitate its success? What changes would need to happen?, etc.

Share the outputs and capture the group's thoughts in the form of a route map to your successful flexible workplace.

Notes

Depending on group size, it might work better to divide into two at the outset and have groups of Dreamers and Critics.

ENCOURAGING FLEXIBLE BEHAVIOUR

SUPPORTING THE CHANGE

EXERCISE 4

Agreeing success criteria

Aim of the exercise
To generate a list of stakeholders, their needs and potential measures of success.

Method
Encourage people to identify all their stakeholders, ie every person or organisation –
internal and external – who has an interest in the outcomes of their activities.

Working in pairs or subgroups, participants should identify the needs of one or two sets
of stakeholders and how those needs might be defined and measured. They should
consider each need, and come up with a measure for that need.

Notes
Use the examples in the next section *Evaluating Success* to prompt discussion if
necessary.

EVALUATING SUCCESS

EVALUATING SUCCESS

PLAN AHEAD

Remember, if you have made a business case for introducing more flexibility, you will want to be able to test whether it has worked in business terms!

Make sure you know how you're going to judge success – and measure it – from the outset.

There are a range of measures you might consider to be indicators of success. Of course these will depend on the type of work your organisation does. They will also be influenced by the driving factors behind your initial move towards flexible working.

Ideally, you want to generate a combination of **quantitative** and **qualitative** measures.

Whatever you decide to measure to demonstrate the impact, make sure you start with a benchmark against which to measure progress. For example, if you want to show its effect on sickness absence, make sure you have comparable figures for sickness absence for the preceding period.

The following pages look at measures for three different areas of the business.

FINANCIAL MEASURES

- Cost of sickness absence
- Cost of turnover (direct costs, eg recruitment agency fees; indirect costs, eg management time)
- Overtime costs
- Productivity gains
- Budget under/overspend
- Bonuses earned
- Cost of office space

ORGANISATIONAL MEASURES

- Staff morale
- Sickness absence (number of days)
- Lateness
- Team effectiveness
- Appraisal outcomes
- Number of accidents
- Administration up-to-date
- Calls and e-mails returned in accordance with targets

CUSTOMER MEASURES

- Reduced complaints
- Increased loyalty
- Repeat business
- Increased satisfaction
- Improved accessibility and/or opening times
- Responsiveness to client needs
- Good client relationships

NOTES

ACTION PLAN

ACTION PLAN

7 STEPS TO A FLEXIBLE WORKPLACE

If you would like to introduce flexible working into your workplace, this chapter is designed to help you think through the steps you need to take to make an effective transition.

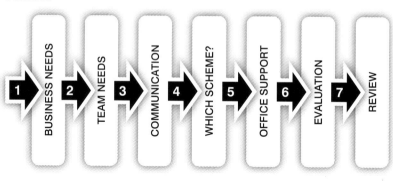

1 BUSINESS NEEDS

2 TEAM NEEDS

3 COMMUNICATION

4 WHICH SCHEME?

5 OFFICE SUPPORT

6 EVALUATION

7 REVIEW

ACTION PLAN

7 STEPS TO A FLEXIBLE WORKPLACE
BUSINESS NEEDS

Examples of issues to consider....

- Are you under pressure to increase productivity?
- Are you aware of demand for different service or opening hours?
- Do you have a high staff turnover?
- Would you like to reduce sickness absence and the costs associated with it?
- Is your office space sufficient for your staff?
- Would you like to reduce overtime payments?
- Can you foresee any potential adverse effect on your service as a result of the scheme?
- Do you make best use of your technology?

1 BUSINESS NEEDS

Think about your business needs and priorities

ACTION PLAN

7 STEPS TO A FLEXIBLE WORKPLACE
TEAM NEEDS

2 **TEAM NEEDS** → Discuss the needs and desires of the individuals within your team →

Examples of issues to consider....

- Do you believe you need to improve morale in your team?

- Are there issues such as stress, absence, lateness, motivation, commitment in the team?

- Do team members have caring responsibilities?

- Do all members of the team want to work more flexibly?

- Has your team discussed its own needs and reached a consensus about the need for change?

- Have everyone's individual needs been acknowledged and respected?

- What benefits have you identified for the team and the individuals within it?

ACTION PLAN

7 STEPS TO A FLEXIBLE WORKPLACE
COMMUNICATION

3 COMMUNICATION → Involve, and communicate with, your staff, colleagues, and clients →

Examples of issues to consider....

- What are your clients and other stakeholders saying? Are you responding to their needs?

- Have you considered the impact of flexible working within your team on other colleagues and consulted them as necessary?

- Is there any need to communicate any changes to external clients?

- Have you identified and dealt with any concerns?

- Have you established a set of principles by which you will all work?

- Do you need to develop or modify your internal communication systems?

ACTION PLAN

7 STEPS TO A FLEXIBLE WORKPLACE
WHICH SCHEME?

4 WHICH SCHEME?

Decide which flexible scheme or schemes to adopt

Examples of issues to consider....

- Have you balanced the business needs with the team's desires to decide which schemes are appropriate and practical?

- Have you considered people's skills and working styles?

- Have you considered whether you need to introduce new or refined work systems?

- Have you reviewed job descriptions to reflect the new way of working?

- Do you or the team need any new skills? If so, are development plans in place?

- Have you ensured contracts of employment are clear? (Discuss with HR/Personnel as necessary.)

ACTION PLAN

7 STEPS TO A FLEXIBLE WORKPLACE

OFFICE SUPPORT

Examples of issues to consider....

- Do you require extended building opening times?

- Have you arranged for the necessary additional office support eg heating, lighting, telephone, security, etc?

- Are you sure the necessary equipment or systems are available eg mobile PCs, time-recording spreadsheets, voicemail, etc?

- Are your internal support services able to operate at the necessary times eg technical support?

- Have you satisfied any necessary health and safety requirements?

- Have any extra associated costs been budgeted for?

5 OFFICE SUPPORT → Ensure you have adequate office support systems in place

ACTION PLAN

7 STEPS TO A FLEXIBLE WORKPLACE
EVALUATION

6 EVALUATION

Consider how you will evaluate the success of your scheme

Examples of issues to consider....

- Have you and your team agreed what success will look like for your flexible workplace scheme?

- Have you established evaluation systems based around those success criteria?

- Have you considered what measurement systems you will use to measure the financial impact?

- Have you considered what measurement systems you will use to measure the cultural impact? eg staff survey

- Have you undertaken a baseline assessment so that you have something against which to measure the business impact of your scheme?

ACTION PLAN

7 STEPS TO A FLEXIBLE WORKPLACE
REVIEW

7 REVIEW → Consider how you will keep your scheme under review →

Examples of issues to consider....

- Have you and your team agreed how you will monitor your flexible workplace scheme on an ongoing basis?

- Do you have a communication mechanism in place specifically for people to make suggestions about the scheme?

- Are you going to operate the new scheme for a trial period and is there an agreed timescale for this?

- Have you agreed what action you will take if you decide the scheme is not working for all or some of the team?

- Have you agreed what action you will take if the scheme is working for the people but not the business?

About the Author

Anne Dickens

Anne works with organisations to help them get the most out of their people. Her working philosophy is be *'people centred but business focused'*. As a consultant and coach specialising in developing people's competence and confidence, she ensures positive results for managers, their teams and the organisations she works with.

She believes in devolving power and responsibility to the person doing the job and has applied this principle to ensure the successful implementation of flexible working projects in the public, private and not for profit sectors.

With a strong conviction that good communication means good business, Anne also works regularly on public relations and internal communications campaigns.

Contact

If you would like Anne to support your move to a more flexible workplace, contact her at: mail@annedickens.co.uk or www.annedickens.co.uk

THE MANAGEMENT POCKETBOOK SERIES

Pocketbooks

Appraisals
Assertiveness
Balance Sheet
Business Planning
Business Writing
Call Centre Customer Care
Career Transition
Challengers
Coaching
Communicator's
Competencies
Controlling Absenteeism
Creative Manager's
C.R.M.
Cross-cultural Business
Cultural Gaffes
Customer Service
Decision-making
Developing People
Discipline
Diversity
E-commerce
Emotional Intelligence
Employment Law

Empowerment
Energy and Well-being
Facilitator's
Flexible Workplace
Handling Complaints
Icebreakers
Impact & Presence
Improving Efficiency
Improving Profitability
Induction
Influencing
International Trade
Interviewer's
I.T. Trainer's
Key Account Manager's
Leadership
Learner's
Manager's
Managing Budgets
Managing Cashflow
Managing Change
Managing Recruitment
Managing Upwards
Managing Your Appraisal

Marketing
Meetings
Mentoring
Motivation
Negotiator's
Networking
NLP
Openers & Closers
People Manager's
Performance Management
Personal Success
Positive Mental Attitude
Presentations
Problem Behaviour
Problem Solving
Project Management
Quality
Resolving Conflict
Sales Excellence
Salesperson's
Self-managed Development
Starting In Management
Strategy
Stress

Succeeding at Interviews
Teamworking
Telephone Skills
Telesales
Thinker's
Time Management
Trainer Standards
Trainer's
Training Evaluation
Training Needs Analysis
Vocal Skills

Pocketsquares

Great Training Robbery
Hook Your Audience

Pocketfiles

Trainer's Blue Pocketfile of
Ready-to-use Activities

Trainer's Green Pocketfile of
Ready-to-use Activities

Trainer's Red Pocketfile of
Ready-to-use Activities

26.5.05

ORDER FORM

Your details

Name _____

Position _____

Company _____

Address _____

_____

_____

Telephone _____

Fax _____

E-mail _____

VAT No. (EC companies) _____

Your Order Ref _____

Please send me:

		No. copies
The _Flexible Workplace_ Pocketbook		☐
The _____ Pocketbook		☐
The _____ Pocketbook		☐
The _____ Pocketbook		☐
The _____ Pocketbook		☐

Order by Post

MANAGEMENT POCKETBOOKS LTD
LAUREL HOUSE, STATION APPROACH, ALRESFORD,
HAMPSHIRE SO24 9JH UK

Order by Phone, Fax or Internet

Telephone: +44 (0)1962 735573
Facsimile: +44 (0)1962 733637
E-mail: sales@pocketbook.co.uk
Web: www.pocketbook.co.uk

Customers in USA should contact:
Stylus Publishing, LLC, 22883 Quicksilver Drive,
Sterling, VA 20166-2012
Telephone: 703 661 1581 or 800 232 0223
Facsimile: 703 661 1501 E-mail: styluspub@aol.com